Waterlight

Also by Kathleen Jamie

POETRY

Black Spiders
A Flame in Your Heart, with Andrew Greig
The Way We Live
The Autonomous Region: Poems and Photographs from Tibet,
with Sean Mayne Smith
The Queen of Sheba
Jizzen
Mr and Mrs Scotland Are Dead: Poems 1980-1994
The Tree House

NONFICTION

The Golden Peak
Among Muslims: Meetings at the Frontiers of Pakistan
Findings: Essays on the Natural and Unnatural World

Waterlight

SELECTED POEMS

Kathleen Jamie

Graywolf Press

SAINT PAUL, MINNESOTA

Poems have been selected from the following books: *The Tree House* (2004) and *Jizzen* (1999), both first published in the United Kingdom by Picador, an imprint of Macmillan Publishers Ltd; and *Mr and Mrs Scotland Are Dead* (2002), published in the United Kingdom by Bloodaxe Books.

Publication of this volume is made possible in part by a grant provided by the Minnesota State Arts Board, through an appropriation by the Minnesota State Legislature; a grant from the Wells Fargo Foundation Minnesota; and a grant from the National Endowment for the Arts, which believes that a great nation deserves great art. Significant support has also been provided by the Bush Foundation; Target; the McKnight Foundation; and other generous contributions from foundations, corporations, and individuals. To these organizations and individuals we offer our heartfelt thanks.

Published by Graywolf Press
2402 University Avenue, Suite 203
Saint Paul, Minnesota 55114
All rights reserved.

www.graywolfpress.org

Published in the United States of America

ISBN 978-1-55597-465-7

2 4 6 8 9 7 5 3 1
First Graywolf Printing, 2007

Library of Congress Control Number: 2006929505

Cover design: Christa Schoenbrodt, Studio Haus

Cover photograph: Sue Colvil, iStockphoto.com

Contents

FROM *The Tree House*

The Wishing Tree	3
Frogs	5
Alder	6
Water Day	7
The Cave of the Fish	9
For When the Grape-vine's Sap	10
Before the Wind	11
Speirin	12
The Bower	13
Swallows	14
The Blue Boat	15
The Glass-hulled Boat	16
White-sided Dolphins	17
Basking Shark	18
The Whale-watcher	20
The Buddleia	21
Hame	22
Pipistrelles	23
Daisies	24
Rhododendrons	25
Moult	26
The Falcon	27
The Tree House	28
The Cupboard	30

The Creel   31

The Brooch   32

The Puddle   33

The Dipper   35

FROM *Jizzen*

Crossing the Loch   39

The Graduates   41

Forget It   43

The Barrel Annunciation   47

The Bogey-wife   48

Ultrasound   49

The Tay Moses   57

Bonaly   59

Mrs McKellar, her martyrdom   60

Flower-sellers, Budapest   62

Song of Sunday   64

Hackit   66

Pioneers   68

Suitcases   69

Lochan   70

Rhododendrons   71

Lucky Bag   73

The Well at the Broch of Gurness   74

St Brides   75

The Green Woman   76

Bolus   77

On the Design Chosen for the
New Scottish Parliament Building
by Architect Enric Miralles 78
Meadowsweet 79

FROM *Mr and Mrs Scotland Are Dead*

Julian of Norwich 83
The Queen of Sheba 85
Hand Relief 89
Child with Pillar Box and Bin Bags 90
Fountain 91
Wee Wifey 92
Outreach 93
Perfect Day 95
Mr and Mrs Scotland Are Dead 96
Arraheids 98
Sky-burial 99
Swallows and Swifts 102
The Sea-house 103
Rooms 105
At Point of Ness 106
Skeins o Geese 108

FROM *The Tree House*

The Wishing Tree

I stand neither in the wilderness
nor fairyland

but in the fold
of a green hill

the tilt from one parish
into another.

To look at me
through a smirr of rain

is to taste the iron
in your own blood

because I hoard
the common currency

of longing: each wish
each secret assignation.

My limbs lift, scabbed
with greenish coins

I draw into my slow wood
fleur-de-lys, the enthroned Britannia.

Behind me, the land
reaches towards the Atlantic.

And though I'm poisoned
choking on the small change

of human hope,
daily beaten into me

look: I am still alive—
in fact, in bud.

Frogs

But for her green
palpitating throat, they lay
inert as a stone, the male
fastened like a package
to her back. They became,

as you looked, almost
beautiful, her back
mottled to leafy brown,
his marked with two stripes,
pale as over-wintered grass.

When he bucked, once,
neither so much as blinked;
their oval, gold-lined eyes
held to some bog-dull
imperative. The car

that would smear them
into one—belly
to belly, tongue thrust
utterly into soft brain—
approached and pressed on.

Oh how we press on—
the car and passengers, the slow
creatures of this earth,
the woman by the verge
with her hands cupped.

Alder

Are you weary, alder tree,
in this, the age of rain?

From your branches
droop clots of lichen

like fairy lungs. All week,
squalls, tattered mists:

alder, who unfolded
before the receding glaciers

first one leaf then another,
won't you teach me

a way to live
on this damp ambiguous earth?

The rain showers
release from you a broken tune

but when the sun blinks, as it must,
how you'll sparkle—

like a fountain in a wood
of untold fountains.

Water Day

For four hours every eight days
our terraces' *acequias*
run with snow-melt,
sufficient for the almond
and orange trees, poppies,
irises, pimpernels.

And whether it's the water's
urgency or the beauty
of its governance, the way
it slakes the clay-
lined channels, its blithe
career through sluice gates;
or the fig tree
swelling over holding tanks
as water spills
through weedy gullets,
oracular and olive-green—

couldn't we make
heavy weather of it all?
Proof of remote
beneficent mountains; the mind's
release from silence, the boll
and eagre of sex, perhaps,
or poetry?

Or we might just follow
the custom hereabouts,

and rise at dawn on water day,
walk a mile in its company
as it falls, level
down to level, till it simply
quits the tenancy of our short lives,
and let it go.

The Cave of the Fish

It winds through sage,
cypresses, rock rose —
the drove road long

shared by goatherds
and fisherfolk. At noon
they'd retreat to a high cave,

seclude their wares
deep in its shade,
talk there, or doze.

Though some of them
had a whiff of the beast,
others a hint of brine,

the path below led home
for both, neither
more true nor more right.

Today I sit at the cave's
cool mouth, halfway
through my life.

For When the Grape-vine's Sap

(efter Hölderlin)

For when the grape-vine's sap
thon canny plant, seeks shedda,
an the grape swells
ablo a caller pend o leaves,
it gies smeddum tae men;
but tae lasses, sweetness
—an bees, steer't wi the speerit
o the sun, bedrucken
wi spring's braith
bummle efter it,
but when the sun beeks,
fey-like, they turn hame

        abune
            the aik reeshles

Before the Wind

If I'm to happen upon the hill
where cherries grow wild
it better be soon, or the yellow-
eyed birds will come squabbling,

claiming the fruit for their own.
Wild means stones barely
clothed in flesh, but that's rich
coming from me. A mouth

contains a cherry, a cherry
a stone, a stone
the flowering branch
I must find before the wind

scatters all trace of its blossom,
and the fruit comes, and yellow-eyed birds.

Speirin

Binna feart, hinny,
yin day we'll gang thegither
tae thae stourie
blaebellwids,
and loss wirsels—

see, I'd raither
whummel a single oor
intae the blae o thae wee flo'ers
than live fur a' eternity
in some cauld hivvin.

Wheest, nou, till I spier o ye
will ye haud wi me?

The Bower

Neither born nor gifted
crafted nor bequeathed
this forest dwelling's little
but a warp or tease

in the pliant light
trees soften and confine.
Though it's nothing
but an attitude of mind

mere breath rising in staves,
the winds assail
its right to exist, this anchorage
or musical box, veiled

and listing deep
in the entailed estate,
sure only of its need
to annunciate.

But when song, cast
from such frail enclaves
meets the forest's edge,
it returns in waves.

Swallows

I wish my whole battened
heart were a property
like this, with swallows
in every room—so at ease

they twitter and preen
from the picture frames
like an audience in the gods
before an opera

and in the mornings
wheel above my bed
in a mockery of pity
before winging it

up the stairwell
to stream out into light

The Blue Boat

How late the daylight edges
toward the northern night
as though journeying
in a blue boat, gilded in mussel shell

with, slung from its mast, a lantern
like our old idea of the soul

The Glass-hulled Boat

First come the jellyfish:
mauve-fringed, luminous bowls
like lost internal organs,
pulsing and slow.

Then in the green gloom
swaying sideways and back
like half-forgotten ancestors
—columns of bladderwrack.

It's as though we're stalled in a taxi
in an ill-lit, odd
little town, at closing time,
when everyone's maudlin

and really, ought just to *go
home*, you sorry inclining
pillars of wrack, you lone,
vaguely uterine jellyfish

—whom I almost envy:
spun out, when our engines churn,
on some sudden new trajectory,
fuddled, but unperturbed.

White-sided Dolphins

When there was no doubt,
no mistaking for water-glint
their dorsal fins'
urgent cut and dive

we grabbed cameras, threw ourselves
flat on the fore-deck. Then,
just for a short time
we travelled as one

loose formation: the muscular
wingers, mothers-with-young,
old scarred outriders
all breached alongside,

took it in turn
to swoon up through our pressure-wave,
careen and appraise us
with a speculative eye

till they'd seen enough,
when true to their own
inner oceanic maps, the animals
veered off from us, north by northwest.

Basking Shark

When I came to the cliff-edge
and lay down, all beneath
was space, then green-
tinted sea, so clear
it revealed, level below level,
not void, but a living creature.

Behind me peat moor
careered inland. I gripped
sweet rock—but it was only
resting, berthed as though
drawn by the cliff's
peculiar backwash,

precisely that its ore-
heavy body and head—
the tail fin measuring back,
forth, like a haunted door—
could come to sense the absolute
limits of its realm.

While it hung, steady
as an anvil but for the fins'
corrective rippling—dull,
dark and buoyed like a heart
that goes on living
through a long grief

what could one do but watch?
The sea heaved; fulmars
slid by on static wings;
the shark—not ready yet
to re-enter the ocean
travel there, peaceable and dumb—

waited, and was watched;
till it all became
unbearable, whereupon the wind
in its mercy breathed again
and far below the surface
glittered, and broke up.

The Whale-watcher

And when at last the road
gives out, I'll walk—
harsh grass, sea-maws,
lichen-crusted bedrock—

and hole up the cold
summer in some battered
caravan, quartering
the brittle waves

till my eyes evaporate
and I'm willing again
to deal myself in:
having watched them

breach, breathe, and dive
far out in the glare,
like stitches sewn in a rent
almost beyond repair.

The Buddleia

When I pause to consider
a god, or creation unfolding
in front of my eyes—
is this my lot? Always
brought back to the same
grove of statues in ill-
fitting clothes: my suddenly
elderly parents, their broken-down
Hoover; or my quarrelling kids?

Come evening, it's almost too late
to walk in the garden, and try,
once again, to retire the masculine
God of my youth
by evoking instead the divine
in the lupins, or foxgloves, or self-
seeded buddleia,
whose heavy horns flush as they
open to flower, and draw
these bumbling, well-meaning bees
which remind me again,
of my father . . . whom, Christ,
I've forgotten to call.

Hame

(efter Hölderlin)

Wha's tae ken
if whiles Ah dauner
yur back-braes, O Yird
and pu wild berries
tae slocken ma luve fur ye
—here whaur jags o roses
and gean-trees
pit oot thur sweet air,
aside the birks, at noon,

when, in the yella glebe
grouin corn reeshles,
and the ickers nod, like at hairst,
—but nou, ablo the aiks' lift,
whaur ah wunner an spier
heivenward, yonner
weel-kent bell jows
gowden notes,
at the oor the birds wauken
ance mair. An a's weel.

Pipistrelles

In the centre of the sheep-field
a stand of Douglas firs
hold between them, tenderly,
a tall enclosure like a vase.

How could we have missed it
before today—never have seen
this clear, translucent vessel
tinted like citrine?

What we noticed were pipistrelles:
cinder-like, friable, flickering
the place hained by trees
till the air seemed to quicken

and the bats were a single
edgy intelligence, testing their idea
for a new form
which unfolded and cohered

before our eyes. The world's
mind is such interstices;
cells charging with light of day—
is that what they were telling us?

But they vanished, suddenly,
before we'd understood,
and the trees grew in a circle,
elegant and mute.

Daisies

We are flowers of the common
sward, that much we understand.
Of everything else
we're innocent. No Creator
laid down such terms
for our pleasant lives,
—it's just our nature,
were we not so,
we wouldn't be daisies, closing
our lashes at the first
suggestion of Venus. By then,
we're near exhausted. Evening
means sleep, and surely it's better
to renew ourselves than die
of all that openness?
But die we will, innocent
or no, of how night
spills above our garden,
twins glittering there
for each of us; die
never knowing what we miss.

Rhododendrons

It wasn't sand martins
hunting insects in the updraught,
or the sudden scent of bog myrtle

that made me pause, lean
across the parapet,
but a handful of purple baubles

reflected below the water's surface
as comfortable and motionless
as a family in their living room

watching TV. What was it,
I'd have asked, to exist
so bright and fateless

while time coursed
through our every atom
over its bed of stones—?

But darkness was weighing
the flowers and birds' backs,
and already my friends had moved on.

Moult

At a certain time of year
come floating shorewards
innumerable seabirds'
primaries and coverts.

Though they're dead things
washed up on the sand
each carries a part
—a black tip, say, to the vane—

of the pattern the outstretched
wing displays. What
can one frayed feather
tell of that design,

or the covenant they undertake,
wind and kittiwake?

The Falcon

To the disused quarry
behind our town the single
peregrine fledged there this May
returns and returns. His father
and mother flown, he must be master
already, of a falcon's skills—
to judge the greenwood
so exquisitely his wing tips
graze not a leaf; to ascend
almost out of the world,
then stoop, snapping a pigeon's neck;
he's discovered
or tenderly been shown
every sheltering niche, for hitherto
God's tempered the wind
to the unmeek hawk, but soon
will come winter. It's here,
his native familiar,
he seeks reassurance,
stepping out of empty air
to a rock ledge so weathered now
it could be natural.
He preens, then closes
his constant eyes. In retreat
he becomes most visible.

The Tree House

Hands on a low limb, I braced,
swung my feet loose, hoisted higher,
heard the town clock toll, a car
breenge home from a club
as I stooped inside. Here

I was unseeable. A bletted fruit
hung through tangled branches
just out of reach. Over house roofs:
sullen hills, the firth drained
down to sandbanks: the *Reckit Lady*, the *Shair as Daith*.

I lay to sleep,
beside me neither man
nor child, but a lichened branch
wound through the wooden chamber,
pulling it close; a complicity

like our own, when arm in arm
on the city street, we bemoan
our families, our difficult
chthonic anchorage
in the apple-sweetened earth,

without whom we might have lived
the long ebb of our mid-decades
alone in sheds and attic rooms,
awake in the moonlit souterrains
of our own minds; without whom

we might have lived
a hundred other lives,
like taxis strangers hail and hire,
that turn abruptly on the gleaming setts
and head for elsewhere.

Suppose just for the hell of it
we flagged one—what direction would we give?
Would we still be driven here,
our small-town Ithacas, our settlements
hitched tight beside the river

where we're best played out
in gardens of dockens
and lady's mantle, kids' bikes
stranded on the grass;
where we've knocked together

of planks and packing chests
a dwelling of sorts; a gall
we've asked the tree to carry
of its own dead, and every spring
to drape in leaf and blossom, like a pall.

The Cupboard

As for this muckle
wooden cupboard carted hither
years ago, from some disused
branch-line station, the other
side of the hill, that takes up
more room than the rest of us
put together, like a dour
homesick whale, or mute sarcophagus—

why is it at *my* place?
And how did it sidle
through the racked,
too-narrow door, to hunker
below these sagging rafters,
no doubt for evermore?

The Creel

The world began with a woman,
shawl-happed, stooped under a creel,
whose slow step you recognize
from troubled dreams. You feel

obliged to help bear her burden
from hill or kelp-strewn shore,
but she passes by unseeing
thirled to her private chore.

It's not sea birds or peat she's carrying,
nor fleece, nor the herring bright
but her fear that if ever she put it down
the world would go out like a light.

The Brooch

All I have is small enough
to be held in one hand—
an agate brooch. It's pierced

like an implement or tool,
perhaps a loom weight.
The agates are brindled,

grey, like carded wool,
or the rings inside a cup, drained,
set to be washed on a table.

Of the woman who pinned it
to her plain coat, only this remains:
her gift, my heirloom, stones.

The Puddle

A week's worth of rain
gathers in swing-parks;
pools in hollow
low-lying fields

give the come-hither
to oystercatchers; curlews
insert like thermometers
their elegant bills.

What is it to lie so
level with the world,
to encourage the eye-
for-the-main-chance

black-headed gulls,
goal-posts, willows,
purple-bellied clouds
to inhabit us, briefly

upside down?
Is it written that we
with some life left,
must stake our souls

upright within us
as the grey-hackled heron
by a pond's rim,
ever forbidding

the setting winter sun
to scald us beautifully
ruby and carnelian?
Flooded fields, all pulling

the same lustrous trick,
that flush in the world's light
as though with sudden love—
how should we live?

The Dipper

It was winter, near freezing,
I'd walked through a forest of firs
when I saw issue out of the waterfall
a solitary bird.

It lit on a damp rock,
and, as water swept stupidly on,
wrung from its own throat
supple, undammable song.

It isn't mine to give.
I can't coax this bird to my hand
that knows the depth of the river
yet sings of it on land.

FROM *Jizzen*

Crossing the Loch

Remember how we rowed toward the cottage
on the sickle-shaped bay,
that one night after the pub
loosed us through its swinging doors
and we pushed across the shingle
till water lipped the sides
as though the loch mouthed 'boat'?

I forget who rowed. Our jokes hushed.
The oars' splash, creak, and the spill
of the loch reached long into the night.
Out in the race I was scared:
the cold shawl of breeze,
and hunched hills; what the water held
of deadheads, ticking nuclear hulls.

Who rowed, and who kept their peace?
Who hauled salt-air and stars
deep into their lungs, were not reassured;
and who first noticed the loch's
phosphorescence, so, like a twittering nest
washed from the rushes, an astonished
small boat of saints, we watched water shine
on our fingers and oars,
the magic dart of our bow wave?

It was surely foolhardy, such a broad loch, a tide,
but we live—and even have children
to women and men we had yet to meet

that night we set out, calling our own
the sky and salt-water, wounded hills
dark-starred by blaeberries, the glimmering anklets
we wore in the shallows
as we shipped oars and jumped,
to draw the boat safe, high at the cottage shore.

The Graduates

If I chose children they'd know
stories of the old country, the place
we never left. I swear

I remember no ship
slipping from the dock,
no cluster of hurt, proud family

waving till they were wee
as china milkmaids
on a mantelpiece,

but we have surely gone,
and must knock
with brass kilted pipers

the doors to the old land:
we emigrants of no farewell
who keep our bit language

in jokes and quotes;
our working knowledge
of coal-pits, fevers, lost

like the silver bangle I lost
at the shows one Saturday,
tried to conceal, denied

but they're not daft.
And my bright, monoglot bairns
will discover, misplaced

among the bookshelves,
proof, rolled in a red tube:
my degrees, a furled sail, my visa.

Forget It

History in a new scheme. I stretch
through hip, ribs, oxter, bursting
the cuff of my school shirt, because
this, Mr Hanning, is me.
Sir! Sir! Sir!
—he turns, and I claim
just one of these stories,
razed places, important as castles,
as my own. *Mum!*

We done the slums today!
I bawled from the glass
front door she'd long desired.
What for? bangs the oven shut,
Some history's better forgot.
                    So how come
we remember the years
before we were born? Gutters
still pocked with fifties rain,
trams cruised dim
street-lit afternoons; war
at our backs. The black door
of the close wheezed
till you turned the third stair
then resounded like cannon.
A tower of bannisters. Nana
and me toiled past windows
smeared in blackout, condemned

empty stone. The neighbours had flitted
to council-schemes, or disappeared . . .

Who were the disappeared? Whose
the cut-throat
razor on the mantelpiece, what man's
coat hung thick with town gas, coal
in the lobby press?
           And I mind
being stood, washed like a dog
with kettle and one cold tap
in a sink plumbed sheer
from the window
to the back midden
as multistoreys rose
across the goods yard,
and shunters clanked
through nights shared
in the kitchen recess bed.

I dreamed about my sister in America
I doot she's dead. What rural
feyness this? Another sibling
lost in Atlantic cloud,
a hint of sea in the rain—
the married in England,
the drunken and the mad,
a couple of notes postmarked Canada,
then mist: but this is a past

not yet done, else how come
our parents slam shut, deny
like criminals: *I can't remember, cannae
mind,* then turn at bay: *Why?*

Who wants to know? Stories
spoken through the mouths
of closes: who cares
who trudged those worn stairs,
or played in now rubbled back greens?
*What happened about my granddad? Why
did Agnes go? How come
you don't know*

that stories are balm,
ease their own pain, contain
a beginning, a middle—
and ours is a long driech
now-demolished street. *Forget it!*
Forget them that vanished,
voted with their feet,
away for good
or ill through the black door
even before the great clearance came,
turning tenements outside-in,
exposing gas pipes, hearths
in damaged gables, wallpaper
hanging limp and stained
in the shaming rain.

History, Mr Hanning.
The garden shrank for winter,
and mum stirred our spaghetti hoops
not long before she started back
part-time at Debenhams
to save for Christmas,
the odd wee
luxury, our first
foreign
holiday.

The Barrel Annunciation

I blame the pail
set under our blocked kitchen rhone
which I slopped across the yard

and hoisted to the butt's
oaken rim seven
or nine times in that spring storm;

so plunging rain upon the rain
held in its deep hooped belly
and triggering, unwittingly

without a counter-act of spillage,
some arcane craft laid
like a tripwire or snare,

lore, which if I'd known,
would have dismissed as dupery
—a crone's trick,

sold to the barren at her cottage door
for a dull coin
or a skirt-length of homespun.

The Bogey-wife

She hoists her thigh over back fences,
her feet squash
worms, hands stained brown as dung.

She flusters hens, looking for babies:
one eye swivelling in the middle of her forehead,
leaves, like the yeti,
the proof of her footprint.

She's simple, gets tangled in the netting
of raspberry groves; but canny—keeps
to the railway wall, the kitchen-midden.

She can *smell* babies, will push
between laundry hung to dry
arms, strong as plum-boughs
twisting into fruit,

and the old wives run her out of town,
some banging pot-lids as others shout
This is private property! Ye've nae right!

But she is charming when cornered,
speaks a nice Scots,
wears a fresh T-shirt
and attractive batik trousers.

Ultrasound

(for Duncan)

i. Ultrasound

Oh whistle and I'll come to ye,
my lad, my wee shilpit ghost
summonsed from tomorrow.

Second sight,
a seer's mothy flicker,
an inner sprite:

this is what I see
with eyes closed;
a keek-aboot among secrets.

If Pandora
could have scanned
her dark box,

and kept it locked—
this ghoul's skull, punched eyes
is tiny Hope's,

hauled silver-quick
in a net of sound,
then, for pity's sake, lowered.

ii. Solstice

To whom do I talk, an unborn thou,
sleeping in a bone creel.

Look what awaits you:
stars, milk-bottles, frost
on a broken outhouse roof.

Let's close the door,
and rearrange
the dark red curtain.

Can you tell the days are opening,
admit a touch more light,
just a touch more?

iii. Thaw

When we brought you home in a taxi
through the steel-grey thaw
after the coldest week in memory
—even the river sealed itself—
it was I, hardly breathing,
who came through the passage to our yard
welcoming our simplest things:
a chopping block, the frost-
split lintels; and though it meant a journey
through darkening snow,
arms laden with you in a blanket,
I had to walk to the top of the garden,
to touch, in a complicit
homage of equals, the spiral
trunks of our plum trees, the moss,
the robin's roost in the holly.
Leaning back on the railway wall,
I tried to remember;
but even my footprints were being erased
and the rising stars of Orion
denied what I knew: that as we were
hurled on a trolley through swing doors to theatre
they'd been there, aligned on the ceiling,
        ablaze with concern
for that difficult giving,
before we were two, from my one.

iv. February

To the heap of nappies
carried from the automatic
in a red plastic basket

to the hanging out, my mouth
crowded with pegs;
to the notched prop

hoisting the wash,
a rare flight of swans,
hills still courying snow;

to spring's hint sailing
the westerly, snowdrops
sheltered by rowans—

to the day of St Bride, the first
sweet-wild weeks of your life
I willingly surrender.

v. Bairnsang

Wee toshie man,
        gean tree and rowan
gif ye could staun
yer feet wad lichtsome tread
granite an saun,
but ye cannae yet staun
sae maun courie tae ma airm
an greetna, girna, Gretna Green

Peedie wee lad
        saumon, siller haddie
gin ye could rin
ye'd rin richt easy-strang
ower causey an carse,
but ye cannae yet rin
sae maun jist courie in
and fashna, fashna, Macrahanish Sand

Bonny wee boy
        peeswheep an whaup
gin ye could sing, yer sang
wad be caller
as a lauchin mountain burn
but ye cannae yet sing
sae maun courie tae ma hert
an grieve nat at aa, Ainster an Crail

My ain tottie bairn
       sternie an lift
gin ye could daunce, yer daunce
wad be that o life itsel,
but ye cannae yet daunce
sae maun courie in my erms
and sleep, saftly sleep, Unst and Yell

vi. Sea Urchin

Between my breast
and cupped hand,
             your head

rests as tenderly
as once I may
             have freighted

water, or drawn
treasure, whole
             from a rockpool

with no premonition
of when next I find one
cast up
             broken.

vii. Prayer

Our baby's heart, on the sixteen-week scan
was a fluttering bird, held in cupped hands.

I thought of St Kevin, hands opened in prayer
and a bird of the hedgerow nesting there,

and how he'd borne it, until the young had flown
—and I prayed: this new heart must outlive my own.

The Tay Moses

What can I fashion
for you but a woven
creel of river-
rashes, a golden
oriole's nest, my gift
wrought from the Firth—

and choose my tide: either
the flow, when, watertight
you'll drift to the uplands—
my favourite hills; held safe
in eddies, where salmon, wisdom
and guts withered in spawn,
rest between moves—that
slither of body as you were born—

or the ebb, when the water
will birl you to snag
on reeds, the river-
pilot leaning over the side:
'Name o God!' and you'll change hands:
tractor-man, grieve, farm-wife
who takes you into her
competent arms

even as I drive, slamming
the car's gears,
spitting gravel on tracks
down between berry-fields,

engine still racing, the door wide
as I run toward her, crying
LEAVE HIM! Please,
it's okay, he's mine.

Bonaly

How did we discover our neat fit?
That critical inch, letting her slip
beneath my right arm, her left
snug on my waist? She had the practised
step of a sword-dance medallist,
and I was sensible, possessed
a Girl Guide uniform
stamped and stamped with badges;

and knew how tight to tie
the maroon cotton strip. Ach
it would all go to hell soon enough,
but just that once, on a school pitch
in a Wimpey scheme in Midlothian,
me and Fiona Murray
could beat all comers, pounding
past our shrieking classmates

with our two heads, three legs
like some abomination
the midwife might have smothered
and for what? All for the greater
glory of Bonaly, our House, denoted
by a red sash and named for a loch
somewhere high in the Pentlands—
a place we could scarcely imagine. *Bonaly!*

Mrs McKellar, her martyrdom

Each night she fills, from the fabled
well of disappointment, a kettle
for her hottie. Lying
in his apportioned bed:
Mr McKellar—annulled
beside his trouser press.

Who mentions, who defers to whom
on matters concerning
redecorating the living room,
milk delivery, the damp
stain spreading on the ceiling

when a word is a kind of touch?
Speaking of which, and they don't,
the garden needs attention
and the bedroom window frames,
exquisitely, the darkening hills,
a sky teased with mauve.

But he won't notice, or smell her burning
fix it! fix it!
won't look up the number
of Roofer and Son about that
slightly bewildering stain,

and she'll keep schtum.
Medieval in a dressing gown,
she'd rather display

toward an indifferent world
the means of her agony:
a broken toilet seat,

or die, lips sealed, regarding
the rotting window sills, that
wobbling shelf, which she could
as it happens, repair herself,
but won't, on principle.

Flower-sellers, Budapest

In the gardens
of their mild southern crofts, their
end-of-the-line hillside vineyards,
where figs turn blue, and peppers dry
strung from the eaves,
old women move among flowers,
each with a worn knife, a sliver
crooked in the first finger
of her right hand—
each, like her neighbours,
drawing the blade
onto the callus of her thumb,
so flowers, creamy dahlias,
fall into their arms; the stems'
spittle wiped on their pinafores.

Then, when they have enough,
the old women
foregather at the station
to await the slow, busy little train
that will take them to the city,
where families drift between mass
and lunch; and they hunker
at bus depots, termini
scented with chrysanthemums,
to pull from plastic buckets
yellows, spicy russets,
the petally nub of each flower
tight as a bee;

and from their pockets, pink ribbon
strictly for the flowers.

We must buy some,
—though they will soon wither—
from this thin-faced
widow in a headscarf, this mother
perhaps, of married daughters
down at the border—
or *this* old woman, sat
among pigeons and lottery kiosks,
who reaches towards us to proffer
the morning's fresh blooms;
or the woman there who calls 'Flowers!'
in several languages—
one for each invasion:

We must buy some,
because only when the flowers are dispersed
will the old women head for home,
each with her neighbours,
back where they came, with their
empty buckets and thick aprons
on a late morning train.

Song of Sunday

A driech day, and nothing to do
bar watch starlings fluchter
over soup bones
left on a plate on the grass.
All forenoon broth-barley, marrowfat peas
swelled in a kitchen jug,
and I soaked stamps, corners
torn from polite white envelopes
in a saucer till they peeled clear,
neither soggy nor still stuck: 'See,
watch and not tear them, wait at peace.'

    There'd aye be women
    in the kitchen, brisket
    lashed in string, tatties
    peeled lovelessly, blinded
    pale and drowned. *See if one*
    now nicked herself
    with a paring knife
    and spellbound, the house froze—
    only now, hacking back in
    through privet and rowan,
    toward my father caught
    mid stretch and yawn,
    my wee sister playing Sindys
    with the girl next door,
    could I wake them
    with something alien

and lovely
as a kiss.

—and we'd be called to eat
what's put in front of us: potatoes, meat
till we could get down, *Please.*
There were African leopards on TV
and *Songs of Praise.* My stamps were dry,
the odd USA, Magyar Poste exotic
among the tuppenny-ha'penny pinks,
the wee lion
rampant in a corner
and after homework I'd have time
to turn to 'Great Britain'
like I'd been shown,
fold and align the edges
with the orderly squares.
Press. 'Bedtime!' *There.*

Hackit

(after a photograph in the museum
of Sault Ste-Marie, Ontario)

For every acre cleared, a cairn's raised:
a woman, staggering, stone
after stone in her hands. Desire's

wiped from her eyes,
who once touched to her face
all the linen a bride might need,

her sister closing
till their hands met, sheets
folded and stowed in the hold,

and the gatherings of land—
Arran, Bute, the Heads of Ayr
parted as the ship sailed.

Snow layers fields, and trees blur.
She stars from a door,
fingers splayed, face

hackit
under the lace mutch
brought from her box.

But they'd still recognize
her accent, when steadily
she told about surviving

their first winter:
the flour barrels, empty,
the last herring, small as her hand.

Pioneers

It's not long ago. There were,
after all, cameras
to show us these wagons and blurred dogs,
this pox of burnt stump-holes
in a clearing. Pioneers;
their remains now strewn
across the small-town
museums of Ontario:
the axe and plough, the grindstone,
the wife by the cabin door
dead, and another sent for.

Suitcases

Piled high in a corner of a second-hand store
in Toronto: of course,
it's an immigrant country. Sometimes

all you can take is what you can carry
when you run: a photo, some clothes,
and the useless dead-weight

of your mother tongue.
One was repaired
with electrician's tape—a trade

was all a man needed. A girl,
well, a girl could get married. Indeed
each case opened like an invitation:

the shell-pink lining, the knicker-
like pockets you hook back
with a finger to look

for the little linked keys.
I remember how each held a wraith
of stale air, and how the assistant seemed

taken aback by my accent;
by then, though, I was headed for home,
bored, and already pregnant.

Lochan

(for Jean Johnstone)

When all this is over I mean
to travel north, by the high

drove roads and cart tracks
probably in June,

with the gentle dog-roses
flourishing beside me. I mean

to find among the thousands
scattered in that land

a certain quiet lochan,
where water liles rise

like small fat moons,
and tied among the reeds,

underneath a rowan,
a white boat waits.

Rhododendrons

They were brought under sail
from a red-tinged east,
carried down gangplanks
in dockers' arms. Innocent
and rare. Their thick leaves
bore a salt-damp gleam,
their blooms a hidden gargle
in their green throats.

Shuddering on trains
to Poolewe, or Arduine,
where the head gardener leaned
across the factor's desk. On a hill
above the sparkling loch
he spoke to his hands,
and terraces were cut,
sites marked, shallow holes dug

before they were turned out.
—Such terribly gentle
work, the grasping of the fat
glazed pots, the fertile
globe of the root-ball
undisturbed, Yunnan
or Himalayan earth
settled with them.

So we step out from their shade
to overlook Loch Melfort
and the bare glens, ready now
to claim this flowering, purple
flame-bright exotica as our own;
a commonplace, native
as language or living memory,
to our slightly acid soil.

Lucky Bag

Tattie scones, St Andra's banes,
a rod-and-crescent Pictish stane,
a field o whaups, organic neeps,
a poke o Brattisani's chips;
a clootie well, computer bits,
an elder o the wee free Kirk;

a golach fi Knoydart,
a shalwar-kemeez;
Dr Simpson's anaesthetics, zzzzzzzzz,
a gloup, a clachan, a Broxburn bing,
a giro, a demo, Samye Ling;

a ro-ro in the gloaming,
a new-born Kirkcaldy
baby-gro; a Free State, a midden,
a chambered cairn—
yer Scottish lucky-bag, one for each wean;
please form an orderly   rabble.

The Well at the Broch of Gurness

Imagine the sails flying like swans,
women hauling infants
as ox-horns bawled,
and door-bars thudding
home in this socket, where a thrush nests.

And slipping away from the rest
—a girl, crossing flagstones
to the sunken well, where, left hand
on the roof's cool rock,
she steps down out of the world.

Perhaps she's there yet, waiting
till they've done their worst
before she drinks, then barefoot
begins her return toward daylight,
where she'll vanish.

The broch's rubble.
Her homestead's lintels tilt
through mown turf.
But we can follow her, descend
below the bright grasses, the beat of surf

step by hewn step, crouching
till our eyes adjust—before we seek
the same replenishing water,
invisible till reached for,
when reached for, touched.

St Bride's

(for Freya)

So this is women's work: folding
and unfolding, be it linen or a selkie-
skin tucked behind a rock. Consider

the hare in jizzen: her leverets' ears
flat as the mizzen of a ship
entering a bottle. A thread's trick;

adders uncoil into spring. Feathers
of sunlight, glanced from a butterknife
quiver on the ceiling,

and a last sharp twist for the shoulders
delivers my daughter, the placenta
following, like a fist of purple kelp.

The Green Woman

Until we're restored to ourselves
by weaning, the skin jade
only where it's hidden
under jewellery, the areolae still tinged,
—there's a word for women like us.

It's suggestive of the lush
ditch, or even an ordeal,
—as though we'd risen,
tied to a ducking-stool,
gasping, weed-smeared, proven.

Bolus

So little of the world is bequeathed
through us, our gifts
instead, are passed among the living
—like words, or the bolus
of chewed bread
a woman presses with her tongue
into the gorgeous open mouth of her infant.

On the Design Chosen for the
New Scottish Parliament Building
by Architect Enric Miralles

An upturned boat
    —a watershed.

Meadowsweet

*Tradition suggests that certain of the Gaelic
women poets were buried face down.*

So they buried her, and turned home,
a drab psalm
hanging about them like haar,

not knowing the liquid
trickling from her lips
would seek its way down,

and that caught in her slowly
unraveling plait of grey hair
were summer seeds:

meadowsweet, bastard balm,
tokens of honesty, already
beginning their crawl

toward light, so showing her,
when the time came,
how to dig herself out—

to surface and greet them,
mouth young, and full again
of dirt, and spit, and poetry.

FROM *Mr and Mrs Scotland Are Dead:*
Poems 1980–1994

Julian of Norwich

Everything I do I do for you.
Brute. You inform the dark
inside of stones, the winds draughting in

from this world and that to come,
but never touch me.
You took me on

but dart like a rabbit into holes
from the edges of my sense
when I turn, walk, turn.

———————

I am the hermit whom you keep
at the garden's end, but I wander.
I am wandering in your acres

where every step, were I
attuned to sense them,
would crush a thousand flowers.

(Hush, that's not the attitude)
I keep prepared a room and no one comes.
(Love is the attitude)

———————

Canary that I am, caged and hung
from the eaves of the world
to trill your praise.

He will not come.
Poor bloodless hands, unclasp.
Stiffened, stone-cold knees, bear me up.

(And yet, and yet, I am suspended
in his joy, huge and helpless
as the harvest moon in a summer sky.)

The Queen of Sheba

Scotland, you have invoked her name
just once too often
in your Presbyterian living rooms.
She's heard, yea
even unto heathenish Arabia
your vixen's bark of poverty, come down
the family like a lang neb, a thrawn streak
a wally dug you never liked
but can't get shot of.

She's had enough. She's come.
Whit, tae this dump? Yes!
She rides first camel
of a swaying caravan
from her desert sands
to the peat and bracken
of the Pentland hills
across the fit-ba pitch
to the thin mirage
of the swings and chute; scattered with glass.

Breathe that steamy musk
on the Curriehill Road, not mutton-shanks
boiled for broth, nor the chlorine stink
of the swimming pool where skinny girls
accuse each other of verrucas.
In her bathhouses women bear
warm pot-bellied terracotta pitchers

on their laughing hips.
All that she desires, whatever she asks
She will make the bottled dreams
of your wee lasses
look like *sweeties.*

Spangles scarcely cover
her gorgeous breasts, hanging gardens
jewels, frankincense; more voluptuous
even than Vi-next-door, whose
high-heeled slippers
keeked from dressing gowns
like little hooves, wee tails
of pink fur stuffed in the cleavage of her toes;
more audacious even than Currie Liz
who led the gala floats
through the Wimpey scheme
in a ruby-red Lotus Elan
before the Boys' Brigade band
and the Brownies' borrowed coal-truck;
hair piled like candy-floss;
who lifted her hands from the neat wheel
to tinkle her fingers
at her tricks
        among the Masons and the elders and the police.

The cool black skin
of the Bible couldn't hold her,
nor the atlas green

on the kitchen table,
you stuck with thumbs
and split to fruity hemispheres—
yellow Yemen, Red Sea, *Ethiopia.* Stick in
with the homework and you'll be
cliver like yer faither,
but no too cliver,
no *above yersel.*

See her lead those great soft camels
widdershins round the kirk-yaird,
smiling
as she eats
avocados with apostle spoons
she'll teach us how. But first

she wants to strip the willow
she desires the keys
                to the National Library
she is beckoning
        the lasses
        in the awestruck crowd . . .

Yes, we'd like to
        clap the camels,
to smell the spice,
admire her hairy legs and
bonny wicked smile, we want to take
PhDs in Persian, be vice

to her president: we want
to help her
        ask some Difficult Questions

she's shouting for our wisest man
to test her mettle:

        Scour Scotland for a Solomon!

Sure enough: from the back of the crowd
someone growls:
                whae do you think y'ur?

and a thousand laughing girls and she
draw our hot breath
                and shout:

THE QUEEN OF SHEBA!

Hand Relief

Whatever happened to friends like Liz,
who curled her legs on a leather settee,
and touched your knee, girl/girl,
as she whispered what the businessmen of Edinburgh
wear beneath their suits—

laughed and hooked her hair back
saying Tuesday, giving some bloke
hand relief, she'd looked up at the ceiling
for the hundredth time that lunch-hour,
and screaming, slammed the other hand down hard
on the panic button; had to stand there
topless in front of the bouncers
and the furious punter, saying
sorry, I'm sorry, it was just a spider . . .

Whatever happens to girls like Liz
fresh out of school, at noon on a Saturday
waiting for her shift at Hotspots
sauna, in a dressing gown
with a pink printed bunny
who follows you to the window
as you look out at the city
and calls you her pal. She says, *you're a real pal.*

Child with Pillar Box and Bin Bags

But it was the shadowed street-side she chose
while Victor Gold the bookies basked
in conquered sunlight, and though
Dalry Road Licensed Grocer gloried and cast
fascinating shadows she chose
the side dark in the shade of tenements;
that corner where Universal Stores' (closed
for modernisation) blank hoarding blocked
her view as if that process were illegal;
she chose to photograph her baby here,
the corner with the pillar box.
In his buggy, which she swung to face her.
She took four steps back, but
the baby in his buggy rolled toward the kerb.
She crossed the ground in no time
it was fearful as Niagara,
she ran to put the brake on, and returned
to lift the camera, a cheap one.
The tenements of Caledonian Place neither
watched nor looked away, they are friendly buildings.
The traffic ground, the buildings shook, the baby breathed
and maybe gurgled at his mother as she
smiled to make him smile in his picture;
which she took on the kerb in the shadowed corner,
beside the post-box, under tenements, before
the bin-bags hot in the sun that shone
on them, on dogs, on people on the other side
the other side of the street to that she'd chosen,
if she'd chosen or thought it possible to choose.

Fountain

What are we doing when we toss a coin,
just a 5p-piece into the shallow dish
of the fountain in the city-centre
shopping arcade? We look down
the hand-rail of the escalator
through two-three inches of water
at a scatter of coins: round, flat, worthless,
reflections of perspex foliage
and a neon sign—FOUNTAIN.
So we glide from mezzanine to ground,
laden with prams, and bags printed
Athena, Argos, Olympus; thinking: now
in Arcadia est I'll besport myself
at the water's edge with kids,
coffee in a polystyrene cup.
We know it's all false: no artesian well
really leaps through strata
fathoms under *Man at C&A*, but
who these days can thrust her wrists
into a giggling hillside spring
above some ancient city?
So we flick in coins, show the children how:
make a wish! What for, in the shopping mall?
A wee stroke of luck? A something else, a nod
toward a goddess we almost sense
in the verdant plastic? Who says
we can't respond; don't still feel,
as it were, the dowser's twitch
up through the twin handles of the buggy.

Wee Wifey

I have a demon and her name is
                WEE WIFEY
I caught her in a demon trap—the household of my skull
I pinched her by her heel throughout her wily transformations
until
      she confessed
                  her name indeed to be WEE WIFEY
and she was out to do me ill.

So I made great gestures like Jehovah: dividing
land from sea, sea from sky,
                  my own self from WEE WIFEY
(*There,* she says, *that's tidy!*)

Now I watch her like a dolly
keep an eye,
        and mourn her:
For she and I are angry/cry
                because we love each other dearly.
It's sad to note
        that without
              WEE WIFEY
I shall live long and lonely as a tossing cork.

Outreach

With a stick in the hot dust
I draw a tenement, a plane, a church:
my country we have no
family fields. In a smoke-choked hut
where a barren wife gave birth
they pat the sackcloth, *sit!*
while hens peck round the sleeping kids
and someone coughs, coughs. *What your family?*

Hunkered in the mean shade
of our compound walls: *Your tits
not big!* Our yard grows
nothing, their constant feet.
At noon, the murderous heat,
I clang the gate: *come back tomorrow.*
Perhaps in my heart of hearts
I lack compassion. I lie

hot nights on a straight bed,
watch crowded stars through mosquito mesh
and talk to Jesus. Moonlight
strikes our metal gate like a silent gong.
Sometimes I wake
to a dog's yelp, a screech of owl,
sometimes, a wide-eyed girl
hugely wrapped in shawls. *What your husband?*

I walk a fine line with the headman,
write home: *One day I'll build a church;*

because I believe in these Lazarus' huts
are secret believers;
and listen in village lanes
of bones and dung for Jesus' name
among the shouts, the bleating goats,
the bursts of dirty laughter.

Perfect Day

I am just a woman of the shore
wearing your coat against the snow
that falls on the oyster-catchers' tracks
and on our own; falls
on the still grey waters
of Loch Morar, and on our shoulders
gentle as restraint: a perfect weight
of snow as tree-boughs
and fences bear against a loaded sky:
one flake more, they'd break.

Mr and Mrs Scotland Are Dead

On the civic amenity landfill site,
the coup, the dump beyond the cemetery
and the 30-mile-an-hour sign, her stiff
old ladies' bags, open mouthed, spew
postcards sent from small Scots towns
in 1960: Peebles, Largs, the rock-gardens
of Carnoustie, tinted in the dirt.
Mr and Mrs Scotland, here is the hand you were dealt:
fair but cool, showery but nevertheless,
Jean asks kindly; the lovely scenery;
in careful school-room script—
The Beltane Queen was crowned today.
But Mr and Mrs Scotland are dead.

Couldn't he have burned them? Released
in a grey curl of smoke
this pattern for a cable knit? Or this:
tossed between a toppled fridge
and sweet-stinking anorak: *Dictionary for Mothers*
M:—Milk, *the woman who worries . . . ;*
And here, Mr Scotland's John Bull Puncture Repair Kit;
those days when he knew intimately
the thin roads of his country, hedgerows
hanged with small black brambles' hearts;
and here, for God's sake, his last few joiners' tools,
SCOTLAND, SCOTLAND, stamped on their tired handles.

Do we take them? Before the bulldozer comes
to make more room, to shove aside

his shaving brush, her button tin.
Do we save this toolbox, these old-fashioned views
addressed, after all, to Mr and Mrs Scotland?
Should we reach and take them? And then?
Forget them, till that person enters
our silent house, begins to open
to the light our kitchen drawers,
and performs for us this perfunctory rite:
the sweeping up, the turning out.

Arraheids

See thon raws o flint arraheids
in oor gret museums o antiquities
awful grand in Embro—
Dae'ye near'n daur wunner at wur histrie?
Weel then, Bewaur!
The museums of Scotland are wrang.
They urnae arraheids
but show o grannies' tongues,
the hard tongues o grannies
aa deid an gaun
back to thur peat and burns,
but for thur sherp
chert tongues, that lee
fur generations in the land
like wicked cherms, that lee
aa douce in the glessy cases in the gloom
o oor museums, an
they arenae letting oan. But if you daur
sorn aboot an fancy
the vanished hunter, the wise deer runnin on;
wheesht . . . an you'll hear them,
fur they cannae keep fae muttering
ye arenae here tae wonder,
whae dae ye think ye ur?

Sky-burial

On the litter I tilt, sweat,
sail the day-blue
iris of sky; my eyes
flick open like a doll's.
Friends, am I heavy? You bear me
under larches in their first green,
pink nipply flowers
                       droop, tease my lips.
Iris leaves rustle, babble of streams.
Your feet seek stones, slip
the water's glassy sheen.
Level me, *steady,* your murmurs
could be   turbanned merchants
in far-flung bazaars,
my arms lashed gently to my side.

Are we there? whispers a child, no,
                 the stone trail twists
I out-stare the blind sky,
         twin hawks
spiral the stair of their airy tower,
king & queen calling
repulsed   bound.

A heather plateau;
travelling winds bring home on their backs
scented oils,
         rotting birds, bog-weeds.
Arenas of peat-lips

speak of forests, old wolves.
Dry lochans reveal
                    deer-spoor
creamy long-bones of trees.

Now friends, women in a ring,
raise your arms
part the blue sky
to a dark pupil; intelligent eye,
        ice-black retina of stars

slip me in.

                And if the child asks,
as you dust your hands,
turn down toward home in the green glen

                where do they go, the dead?
                    Someone at last
may crack a small joke,

one say she feels watched;
one tug soft arching branches
over the burn.

You may answer him:
            here,   here,

                                    here.

Midsummer on the high moor
my eyes flick open:
                    bouquets
of purple iris, midnight
cathedrals of sky.

The wind unravels me
winter birds will arrive.

Swallows and Swifts

Twitter of swallows and swifts:
'tickets and visas, visas and tickets'—
winter, and cold rain
clears the milky-way of birdshit
where wires cross the lane.

The Sea-house

In this house
are secret rotting wings,
wrecked timbers; the cupboard
under the stair
glimmers with pearl.

The sea-house
rises from dulse; salt winds
boom in its attics. Here:
my tottering
collections of shells, my ballroom
swirling with fulmars.

Morning brings
laundries of wrack,
a sea-maw's grief-shaped wing. Once
a constellation
of five pink buoys.

This place is a stranger's.
Ewers in each high room
hold a little salt water.
My musical box
is a tinkling crab.

The sea-house is purdah:
cormorants' hooked-out wings
screen every chamber. Inside

the shifting place, the
neither-nor

I knock back and forth
like the tongue of a bell
mournfully tolling
in fog, or lie
as if in a small boat
adrift in an upstairs room.

Rooms

Though I love this travelling life and yearn
like ships docked, I long
for rooms to open with my bare hands,
and there discover the wonderful, say
a ship's prow rearing, and a ladder
of rope thrown down.
Though young, I'm weary:
I'm all rooms at present, all doors
fastened against me;
but once admitted start craving
and swell for a fine, listing ocean-going prow
no man in creation can build me.

At Point of Ness

The golf course shifts
uneasily beside the track
where streetlight melts
to a soft frontier with winter dark.
I cross, then, helpless as a ship,
must let night load me, before
moving on between half-sensed
dry-stane walls; day-birds tucked in some nook.

Tonight, the darkness roars.
Even the fishermen's
Nissen hut seems to breathe
beside its spawn of creels,
a dreadful beaching. I walk on,
toward the shore, where night's
split open, the entire
archipelago set as sink-weight
to the sky. A wind's

caught me now; breath frosts,
and I count, to calm me, the Sound's
lighthouses as they shine and fade
across the surge. Graemsay
beams a long systolic five
to one of dark; Hoy a distant
two: two; scattered buoys
blink where skerries drown, then cut
to sea and stars, then
bloom again, weird lilies

wilt and bloom, till,
heart-scared, I have it
understood:

    never   *ever*
harm—this,

            you never could

and run—that constant roar,
the track's black vein; toward salt
lit windows, my own door . . .

                  Sunshine
gleams the dry-stane dykes'
lovely melanoma of lichen. A wren
flicks on a weathered post
like a dud lighter, by the track
that splits the golf course
from the town's edge to the shore,
where I walk this afternoon
for a breath of air.

Skeins o Geese

Skeins o geese write a word
across the sky. A word
struck lik a gong
afore I wis born.
The sky moves like cattle, lowin.

I'm as empty as stane, as fields
ploo'd but not sown, naked
an blin as a stane. Blin
tae the word, blin
tae a' soon but geese ca'ing.

Wire twists lik archaic script
roon a gate. The barbs
sign tae the wind as though
it was deef. The word whustles
ower high for ma senses. Awa.

No lik the past which lies
strewn aroun. Nor sudden death.
No like a lover we'll ken
an connect wi forever.
The hem of its goin drags across the sky.

Whit dae birds write on the dusk?
A word niver spoken or read.
The skeins turn hame,
on the wind's dumb moan, a soun,
maybe human, bereft.

KATHLEEN JAMIE was born in the west of Scotland in 1962. Her poetry collections include *The Tree House* (Picador, 2004), which won the Forward prize and the Scottish Book of the Year Award; *Jizzen* (Picador, 1999), which won the Geoffrey Faber Memorial Award; and *Waterlight: Selected Poems* (Graywolf Press, 2007). *Mr & Mrs Scotland Are Dead* (2002) was shortlisted for the International Griffin Poetry Prize, and in 2002 Jamie was awarded a Creative Scotland Award. A part-time lecturer in Creative Writing at St Andrews University, Kathleen Jamie lives with her family in Fife.

Waterlight has been set in Adobe Caslon Pro, an open type version of a typeface originally designed by William Caslon sometime between 1720 and 1766. The Adobe version was drawn by Carol Twombly in 1989.

Book design by Wendy Holdman.
Composition by Prism Publishing Center.
Manufactured by Versa on acid-free paper.

← barcode